Pandas
For Kids

Amazing Animal Books
for Young Readers

by John Davidson

Mendon Cottage Books

JD-Biz Publishing

Read More Amazing Animal Books

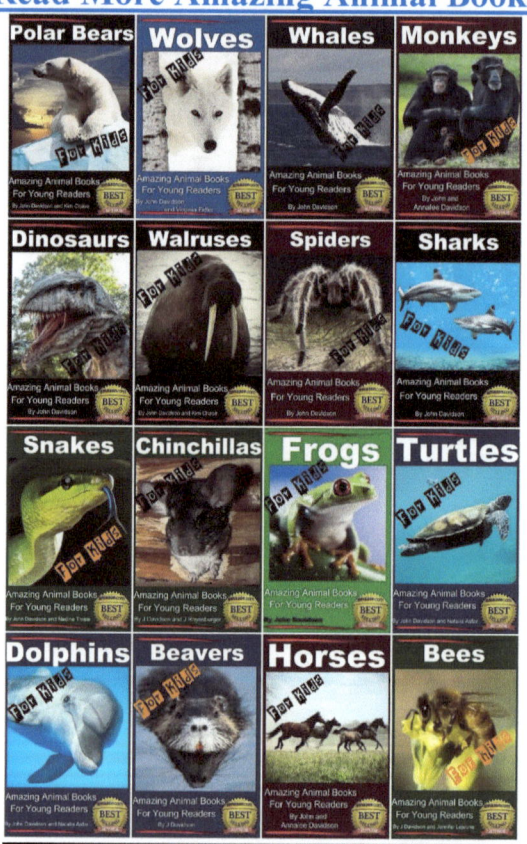

Purchase at Amazon.com
Download Free Books!
http://MendonCottageBooks.com

Table of Contents

1. 10 Facts About Pandas

The following are ten facts about pandas:

1. There are less than 10 million pandas in the world.

2. A panda's hand has six digits as five fingers as well as an opposable thumb.

3. Pandas are found mostly in mountain ranges in central Shaanxi, China's Sichuan, and Gansu provinces.

4. Pandas inhabit mostly mountain forests, which are dense with conifers and bamboo.

5. Due to their ineffective intestinal system, the giant pandas have to feed for approximately 15 hours each day, with bamboo making 99 % of their diet.

6. Giant pandas are among the few bear species that do not hide. This is because it cannot store adequate fat from its diet.

7. Pandas live at high altitudes of about 1,500 to 3,000M. Their thick and oily fur aids keep them warm.

8. Male pandas are called as boars while females are sows. Pandas are solitary creatures.

9. At birth time an infant panda is about 1/900th its mother's body size.

10. The panda is friendly to children compared to adults

2. What Are Pandas Bears?

It is the world's most famous bear! However nothing is simple for the Giant Panda: long forgotten in the mountains of China, it is endangered in only a century and a half after being discovered ... Scientists have long argued over whether this animal is a bear or not ... or a very large raccoon bear cousin. Today they agree that it is a bear. The Chinese for their part call them "bear cats".

Big beefy but squint under his thick coat that allows it to withstand the harsh climate of the mountains, the giant panda is a sturdy. It can weight to one hundred pounds and can stand up to 1.65 meters. It has a good sense of smell, which enables it, among other things, to easily locate his peers, but his vision is not as good as ours.

In the wild the giant panda lives in certain parts of China. Many can be found throughout the region of Sichuan and eastern Tibet. It hides in the mountain forests, where it can live up to 500 meters. A legendary animal The Chinese knew the panda long and had a legendary animal sometimes venturing into the villages to lick kitchen utensils and look for food. For European travelers, it was an imaginary animal until a French missionary, Father Armand David, captures one in 1869. China is celebrating this year the 144th anniversary of the discovery of "official" of its iconic animal. We can now safely say that the panda is really a bear a cute bear that is.

3. Types Of Pandas

Types of panda :

There are actually two different kinds of Panda bear. There are Giant panda bear and Lesser Panda.

Giant panda :

It is also known as black & white panda. It lives in bamboo forests in central china. Currently 14 city zoos outside china have giant pandas. The main food source for this panda is bamboo. They may eat other foods such as honey, eggs, fruits etc. They have white hair on their bodies and black hair on their legs and shoulders. Giant pandas are about 1.5 meter long,75 cm high and 75-150 kilogram weight. Giant pandas live around 20 years. They can Climb and swim well.

Lesser Panda :

It is also Known as Red panda. It's considerably smaller than Giant panda. It lives in southern part of china, Nepal, Himalayan Mountains in high trees. They have red color hair on whole body and their faces have some white designs. They are about 50-60 centimeter long and three to five kilogram weight. It eats fruits, roots, bamboo shoots, insects and various plants. It is active at night and sleep on tree at daytime.

4. Endangered Pandas

A Panda is one of the world's most popular endangered animal. In most parts of the world, Panda's survival is endangered mainly by loss of habitat that relates to economic as well as population growth.

Poaching is another big threat to their survival.

Pandas so dislike human beings association, so they would rather starve than crossing a populated area looking for fresh food source. This is why pandas are so vulnerable to most bamboo vegetation especially after fresh blooming.

The gradual decrease in reproductive rate also threatens their population growth. Inbreeding is another endangering problem since it makes it difficult for most pandas to reproduce and increases vulnerability to disease.

Surviving pandas are doing quite well as most of the government efforts have always to conserve this amazing bear species through creation of parks and museums, burning of poaching, and citizen's education on Panda's importance among other measures on how to conserve this endangered species.

5. Panda Bears Habitat

Panda bears are loved world over by children and toy makers. Their bodies are covered with fur which acts as a source of heat since they live in cold mountainous places. They have a black and white color that blends easily with the mountain terrain helping them camouflage from their predators and their enemies.

The panda bears are only found in limited areas of China and they have been put under the World Wildlife Fund since they are a rare species. Panda bears are excellent tree and rock climbers as an adaptation to their habitat and feed on bird and small animals.

The Panda bears are cute and cuddly to look at. They are however dangerous when provoked. They love privacy and can be easily seen during the mating or nurturing period. Pandas bears are definitely amazing to look at due to their unique and mysterious markings on their skin.

6. Where Do Pandas Live

Panda's survival is limited to specific weather conditions since it is an endangered animal species. They are mostly found in mountainous places with a lot of bamboo forest. Pandas also dislike human beings association, so they have to live a solitary life in these dense and thick forests with many fresh vegetation as their foods.

There are a rare different panda's species, but most common Panda called referred the Giant Panda. Forest clearing for human being settlement as well as farming has made these Giant Panda to live only in a few select mountain ranges found in countries like China. Sichuan in the southwestern China is the Giant Pandas main habitation while other lives in northwestern provinces Shaanxi and Gansu.

Since Pandas have fur on their bodies, they can also be found on winter climates with intense cold. Currently there are approximately three thousand giant Pandas living in incarceration around the world.

7. What Do Panda Bears Eat

Nearly all the species of panda such as Qinling, Red, and Giant, eat predominately bamboo vegetation with approximately 99% of their diet consisting of diverse bamboo species.

Pandas eat nearly all part of bamboo vegetation including the leaves, shoots, and stems. It is supposed that they eat diverse species as well as part of the bamboo with an aim of getting proper food nutrition from it. Pandas always eat large amounts of bamboo every day since it has very low nutritional value.

Since Pandas are unable to digest efficiently the cellulose contained in bamboo, it means they must consume between 20-40 pounds that is 12-38 kg to satisfy their energy needs. Most Pandas eat between 11 to 16 hours a day to put up with them. One% of a Pandas diets is made up of plants as well as meats like fish, pika, insects, and small rodents. They also sometimes eat roots, grasses, fruits, berries, and honey.

8. Giant Panda Bear Behavior

Giant Panda bear behavior

The giant panda bear comes from the bear family and usually is recognized through the white and black patches. The giant panda lives in mountain ranges in china after being displaced from the lowland areas due to forest clearing and farming thereby making the pandas to migrate to the mountains ranges.

Another fascinating giant panda bear behavior is its source of food. The giant panda's feed on bamboo. Bamboo is not easily digestible and has low nutrients. Funny enough, the giant panda bear has to eat lots of it so as to get enough nutrients. The giant panda bear will at times eat berries, meat, flower, nuts and grass to substitute its main food; bamboo. Often the female giant panda bear will give birth to two young ones but will take care of only one while she lets the other to die. After about a year, the young one will be left to live without the mother.

9. Giant Panda Bear Anatomy

Can you be able to describe the giant panda bear anatomy? It may sound strange to you but giant panda has a distinct anatomy that you can use in describing it. Here are basics about the giant panda anatomy.

1. The male panda bears can measure up to 6 feet in length from their nose to the end of the tail.

2. They can weigh approximately 350 pounds, the female are 20% less than the male in body weight.

3. Their body is covered by a heavy fur comprising of two layers. Their fur is oily to serves the purpose of protecting the pandas against the cool climate and repelling water.

5. They have ears that are black in color and round in shape and eye patches are black. The pupils in the eyes have vertical slits like those found in various nocturnal animals. These pupils allow the panda to have an excellent night vision.

6. They have large molar teeth and strong jaws .Their molar teeth are the largest among the mammals.

7. They have a black band across the shoulders and legs that are black.

10. Giant Panda Bear Predators

What are some of the Giant Panda Bear predators? Giant panda predators have contributed greatly to the reduced survival of pandas on earth. The number of pandas is shockingly low .If an action is not taken to protect this animals then soon they will be extinct .From the recent statistics of pandas it was found out that they are very few. The major contributor to the small number of the pandas surviving on earth is the predators which readily kill the pandas for food.

The following are well known predators of panda

Jackals: This hunt on pandas for food. By feeding on the pandas they reduce the population of the pandas greatly.

Leopards: They readily prey on pandas for food. This is a dangerous predator of the pandas considering its high speed as it can run faster hence catching the pandas easily.

Yellow-throated martens: These specialize on killing the cubs of pandas. This contributes greatly to the small number of pandas in the world.

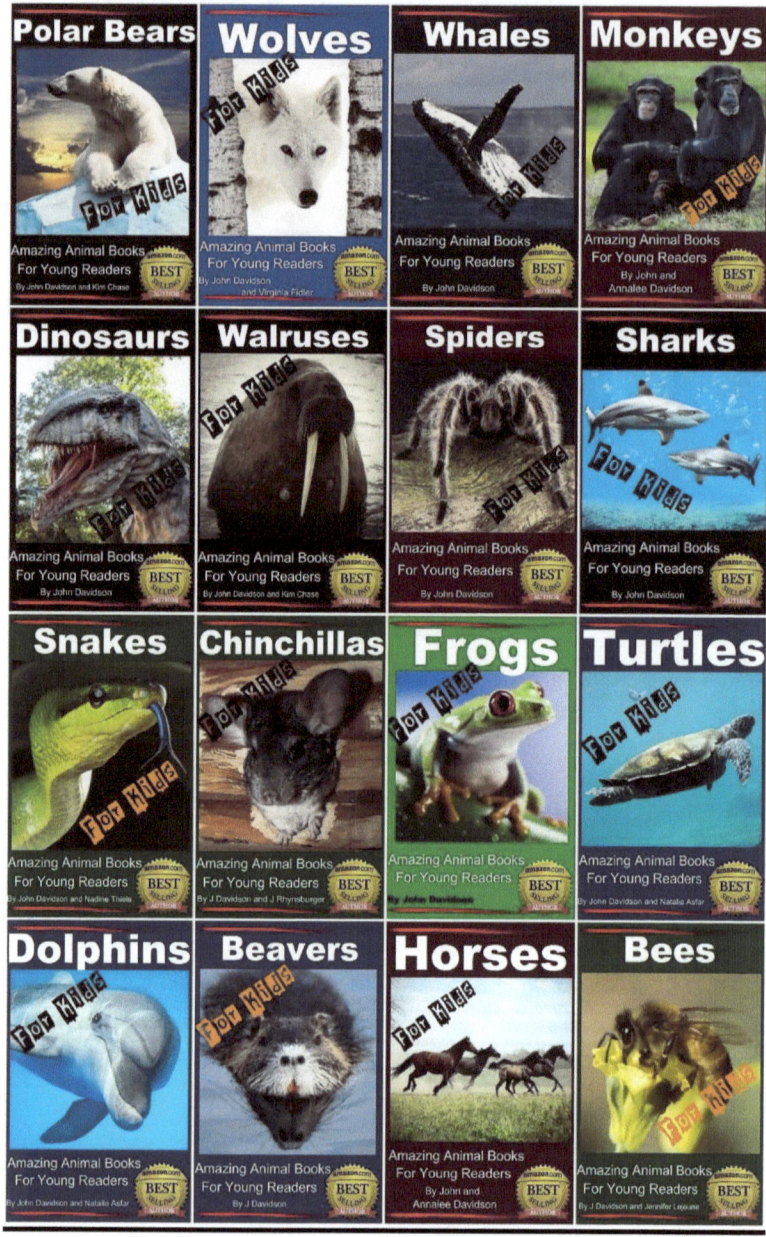

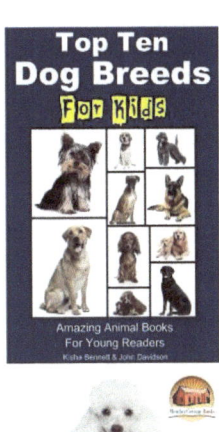

Top Ten Dog Breeds For Kids

Amazing Animal Books For Young Readers

Kisha Bennett & John Davidson

German Shepherds

Dog Books for Kids

K. Bennett

Bulldogs

Dog Books for Kids

K. Bennett

Dachshund

Dog Books for Kids

K. Bennett

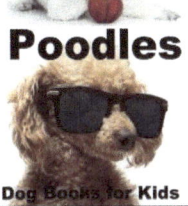

Poodles

Dog Books for Kids

K. Bennett

Labrador Retrievers

Dog Books for Kids

K. Bennett

Rottweilers

Dog Books for Kids

K. Bennett

Boxers

Dog Books for Kids

K. Bennett

Golden Retrievers

Dog Books for Kids

K. Bennett

Puppies

Dog Books For Kids

Amazing Animal Books

By John Davidson

Beagles

Dog Books for Kids

K. Bennett

Yorkshire Terriers

Dog Books for Kids

K. Bennett

Dogs

Top Ten Dog Breeds For Kids

Amazing Animal Books For Young Readers

Zahra Jazeel & John Davidson

Cats For Kids

Amazing Animal Books For Young Readers

K. Bennett & John Davidson

Foxes For Kids

Amazing Animal Books For Young Readers

Zahra Jazeel & John Davidson

Wolves For Kids

Amazing Animal Books For Young Readers

By John Davidson and Virginia Fidler

Our books are available at

1. Amazon.com
2. Barnes and Noble
3. Itunes
4. Kobo
5. Smashwords
6. Google Play Books

Download Free Books!
http://MendonCottageBooks.com

Publisher

JD-Biz Corp

P O Box 374

Mendon, Utah 84325

http://www.jd-biz.com/